Astrology as Business

An Entrepreneur's Guide to Launching a Successful Astrology Service

Table of Contents

Chapter 1. Introduction

Dive into the cosmos and navigate the alignment of entrepreneurship and astrology with our special report: "Astrology as Business: An Entrepreneur's Guide to Launching a Successful Astrology Service." This comprehensive guide isn't just about zodiac signs and the moon's phases—it's about identifying your entrepreneurial North Star and launching a spiritual business that's both personally fulfilling and financially successful. Regardless of your experience, from seasoned astrologers to business-minded novices, our report is designed to enlighten and inspire, detailing practical, step-by-step methods to help you establish, promote, and monetize your astrology services effectively. Who knows? Your future business success might just be written in the stars!

Chapter 2. Unveiling the Astrology Market: An Overview

The study, practice, and belief in celestial events impacting the human world is not alien. Astrology has been an integral part of various cultures around the world, feeding a sense of wonder and curiosity towards the cosmic fabric linking us to the universe at large. While its critical reception varies, one thing remains consistent - astrology's influential presence in business and entrepreneurial arenas.

2.1. The Astrological Landscape

An understanding of the market begins with examining the terrain, which for astrology, is deeply intertwined with personal beliefs and spiritual practices. It's important to note that many individuals engage with astrology as a form of sanctuary, seeking solace and guidance amidst life's uncertainties. For these individuals, astrology represents a comforting structure, offering insightful interpretations about their life paths and relationships. They benefit from a reassuring feeling of cosmic connectivity that provides context to their experiences, giving life's randomness a sense of order and intention.

In terms of age demographics, astrology finds its avid practitioners and followers mainly among the millennial and Gen Z populations, although older generations participate as well. These demographics not only find comfort in its teachings but also enjoy a social bonding aspect through sharing horoscopes, star sign traits, and zodiac compatibility. Millennials in particular, navigating a world marked by an uncertain economy, climate change worries, and political polarities, find in astrology a safe, spiritual haven. This insight into your customer base is invaluable – understanding the demographics as well as the emotional and mental states of your potential clientele underpins much of your venture's success.

2.2. The Market Size

Numerous reports suggest that the astrology market is a booming one. Not only does it have a broad global reach, but the internet has made it easier for astrology services to be provided remotely, closely aligning with the current trend of digitization and remote services. This broadening virtual footprint corresponds to escalated growth in the market size.

A 2019 market research report from IBISWorld states that the Astrology, Mediums, and Psychic Services industries in the US have combined to create a multi-billion dollar market, exhibiting a 2.0% annual growth between 2014 and 2019. This kind of statistics signals a promising opportunity for entrepreneurs in the field.

2.3. Emerging Trends

Given the hybrid nature of this field - perched on the crossroads of spirituality, personal growth, and entertainment - there are several avenues for business expansion. Notable emerging trends include:

1. Technological innovations for personalized astrology experiences.

2. Inclusion of astrology themes in lifestyle products and services, such as clothing, home decor, stationery, and wellness.

3. Astrology-based dating and relationship services.

4. "Spiritual tourism" incorporating astrology into travel experiences.

5. Enhancements in astrology software for more accurate,

comprehensive readings.

Keeping an eye on and adapting to these trends is critical. They provide clues towards future pivot points in the industry, enabling you to architect your services to be in step with the needs and desires of your target clientele.

2.4. Integrating Astrology and Business

While the prospect of turning a spiritual practice into a profitable venture may seem daunting, it's important to remember that success lies at the intersection of passion and service. In essence, your mission should be twofold: to build a thriving business while providing a meaningful, beneficial service that aids personal growth and self-understanding for your clientele.

Some practical steps could serve as a roadmap:

1. Understand your clientele and their needs, as well as the general atmospheric trends influencing their behavior and decisions.
2. Create a unique selling proposal (USP) that will differentiate your services from the competition and make your business stand out.
3. Innovate a digital strategy that is in sync with the current digital norms, emphasizing on consistent, engaging online presence through social platforms and SEO-friendly content.
4. Set fair but profitable price points for your services.
5. Consider collaborating with complementary businesses and influencers for mutual growth and exposure.

2.5. Navigating Challenges

Like any business, embarking on an entrepreneurial journey in the astrology field comes with its set of challenges. Skepticism about astrology's credibility, regulatory policies in different regions, and managing competitive market pressures are a few. But, equipped with a thorough understanding of the business terrain, in-depth market analysis, and an innovative, adaptable strategy, the prospect of establishing a successful astrology service becomes a reality - not merely a constellation of distant dreams.

Endeavoring to seize this unique niche, remember: you are not merely selling a service or a product but are facilitating a means for people to self-explore and self-understand, to find comfort and guidance, to wonder and wander among the cosmos - within and without.

A successful astrology business isn't merely about finding your North Star, but about lighting the path for others to discover theirs. Launching into the astrology market offers an extraordinary entrepreneurial journey, where the science of business strategy aligns with the spirituality of heavenly bodies, casting a unique, radiant glow on the path to prosperity.

Chapter 3. Threading the Cosmic Needle: Identifying Your Astrology Niche

In a market as broad and varied as the astrology services industry, finding your unique place is tantamount to a spacecraft plotting its trajectory through the cosmos. Knowing your astrology niche ensures you stay pointed at your North Star and not swept by the current of competition. Like threading a needle in the cosmos, finding your niche can be daunting yet deeply rewarding once identified and pursued with intent.

3.1. Understanding Your Audience

Before you decide on your niche, you should first understand your potential clients' aspirations, wants, expectations, and fears. These factors will guide you in formulating astrology services that resonate and connect deeply with your clientele.

Start by defining the demographics of your target market, such as their age, gender, income level, education, and location. Are they high-income individuals seeking astrological advice on business decisions? Or are they young educated adults looking for spiritual guidance and self-discovery?

Exploring psychographics is equally essential. Dive into their lifestyles, interests, values, and opinions. Maybe your audience finds solace in spirituality amidst their hectic modern lifestyles. Or perhaps, they value knowledge and understanding, seeking astrological readings to feed their curiosity about life and the universe.

3.2. Unearth Your Unique Strengths

The astrology industry is incredibly diverse, with many astrologers offering a wide array of services. Some offer horoscope readings, others provide birth chart interpretations, while others focus on predictive astrology. Understanding your unique strengths, combined with your knowledge of your target audience, is pivotal in finding your niche.

If your strength is predicting business trends using astrology, your clientele might be business-minded individuals who value strategic endeavors guided by celestial insights. Suppose you are proficient at understanding personal relationships through astrology. In that case, your services might resonate most with individuals seeking insights into their personal relationships.

3.3. Monitor Market Trends

In navigating the cosmos of today's dynamic business world, being attuned to market trends is crucial. Just as the cosmos is a shifting sea of celestial bodies, the market changes and adapts to the evolving needs and interests of consumers.

With celestial movements as your guide, identify the ebb and flow of the astrology market. Are there emerging trends that your audience resonates with? Are there untapped areas of the market? By aligning your strengths with the trends, you increase your chance of finding a niche that is both relevant and profitable.

3.4. Develop Your Unique Service Offering

Once you have gathered insights about your audience, understood your strengths, and monitored market trends, it's time to develop your unique service offering.

If your strength is in predictive astrology and your audience are businesses, maybe offer personalized celestial business forecasts. Or, if you resonate more with relationship astrology and your target market is individuals seeking relationship advice, tailor your services providing astrological insights into relationships.

3.5. Refine and Pivot as Necessary

No astrologer starts out perfectly attuned to the energies of their target audience. Finding your niche is a practice of ongoing refinement, continual learning, and sometimes, pivoting.

Remember, like planets and stars, markets move, and the needs and interests of your audience evolve. Staying reflective, open to feedback, and flexible allows you to adapt and grow your business successfully.

When you thread the cosmic needle correctly, finding your niche fuels your astrology business's success. With alignment and patience, you can navigate your business to engage with your clientele in meaningful and rewarding ways. Then, you harness the cosmos's energy to illuminate the path of entrepreneurship, an eternal dance between you, your clients, and the cosmic tapestry that binds us all.

Chapter 4. Building Your Astral Identity: Branding in the Astrology Business

Brand recognition is a powerful catalyst for business growth in any industry, the astrology sector notwithstanding. In this cosmic journey we're embarking on, your "Astral Identity"—which refers to your branding in the astrology business—is your spacecraft. It is the beacon that paves the way through the vast entrepreneurial cosmos and draws your potential clients towards your unique services. Establishing a potent and distinguishable astral identity sets you apart from others, ensuring that your stellar services attract those seeking guidance from the stars.

4.1. The Importance of an Astral Identity

The Astrology sector has seen significant growth over the last decade, with countless entrepreneurs offering various spiritual and astrology services. Amid this crowded cosmic market, why should customers choose your services? The answer lies in your astral identity — your distinct character that resonates with your target audience and echoes your values, expertise, and the unique stellar journey you offer.

Understanding the significance of a strong astral identity is the first step towards its effective establishment. A memorable brand fosters trust, creates emotional connections, and simplifies the customer's decision-making process, guiding them towards your services when they seek astrological insights.

4.2. Crafting Your Unique Astral Story

Identifying your astral story requires self-exploration, introspection, and an acute understanding of your passion for astrology. This story will act as the foundation for your astral identity. Here, your personal journey, understanding, and passion for astrology will weave together to form a compelling narrative that sets you apart.

To establish this, think about:

1. What led you to astrology?

2. What makes your approach unique?

3. Which astrological aspects stir your interest the most?

4. How has astrology transformed your life and perception, and how do you wish it to impact others?

Your astral story should emanate authenticity and passion, resonating with your potential clients—those who share similar interests or are seeking the insights you can provide.

4.3. Creating an Astral Identity Visual Element

Visuals play a crucial role in creating a lasting impression. For your astral identity, this includes everything from your logo and color scheme to the images you use in promoting your services.

Consider the following elements while designing your astral identity:

1. Logo: A visually appealing, easy-to-remember design capturing the essence of your astral story

2. Color Palette: Colors associated with your story. If your focus is

on lunar astrology, shades of silver and navy may be apt. Solar signs might align with gold and red.

3. Imagery: High-quality images depicting celestial bodies, astrological signs, or anything that relates to your unique astral story

4. Typography: Engaging and attractive fonts that align with your overall design

Remember, consistency in visual elements across all platforms strengthens brand recall, aiding in building a strong astral identity.

4.4. Establishing Your Astral Voice

The tone, language, and overall style of communication constitute your astral voice. Align this with your astral story and the audience you aim to resonate with. You might want a mystical tone for a deeply spiritual audience or a conversational one for novices. The key is consistency so that your audience can become familiar with, and grow to trust, your voice.

4.5. Conveying Your Expertise and Credibility

Your astral identity must convey your expertise and understanding of astrology clearly. Share your qualifications, courses completed, years of practice, testimonials, or anything highlighting your proficiency and the results clients can expect, lending credibility to your astral identity.

4.6. The Impact of a Strong Astral Identity

Well-defined astral identities break through the noise in the astrology market, successfully attracting potential clientele while forming strong emotional bonds. Through their potency, they generate unstoppable momentum propelling the business closer to its stellar aspirations.

Revisit your astral identity from time to time, ensuring it continues to resonate with you and your audience while reflecting your growth and the evolution of your services. Creating an astral identity is not a one-time event, but a continuous process that aligns with your unique contributions to astrology.

In essence, your astral identity is the guiding star for your entrepreneurial journey. Craft it with passion, authenticity, and dedicated consistency, illuminating the path for yourself and those seeking your guiding light in the cosmic expanse of the astrology business.

Chapter 5. All Systems Go: Setting up Your Astrology Business

Beginning your journey as an entrepreneur in the field of astrology is a decision that promises personal fulfillment and financial success. However, moving forward in the right direction requires strategic planning and preparation in various areas. This part of the guide focuses on setting up your astrology business, taking you through a systematic and exhaustive approach that incorporates all the necessary aspects.

5.1. The Business Plan

Every entrepreneurial journey begins with a robust business plan. This blueprint outlines your business's strategic roadmap, including your mission, vision, operational strategies, financial forecast, marketing plan, and much more.

Define your business's purpose: Why are you starting an astrology business? Are you looking to help people understand themselves or their futures better? This purpose will be your guiding light through your entrepreneurial journey.

Financial Projections: Depict anticipated financial performance for the next 3 to 5 years. Take into account both your projected income and expenses, such as website hosting, software purchases, marketing, and promotions.

Competitor Analysis: Identify your main competitors. What is their business model? What are their strengths and weaknesses? How can you differentiate your services?

Marketing and Sales Strategy: How will you attract and retain customers? This could range from online content marketing to paid advertisements or word-of-mouth referrals. Your sales strategy might detail how you plan to price your services or outline a strategy for selling add-on products or services.

5.2. Legal Considerations and Registrations

Running a successful astrology business requires compliance with local laws and regulations. Here are some legal aspects you should consider:

Business Structure: Should you register as a sole proprietorship, partnership, LLC, or corporation? The right choice depends on your financial situation and liability concerns.

Tax Registrations: Research the tax regulations in your area. You will likely need to register for a tax ID and understand which business expenses you can write off.

Licenses and Permits: Depending on your location, you may need specific licenses or permits to operate an astrology business.

Privacy Policies: If you are collecting client's personal data (e.g., birth dates), a clear privacy policy is essential.

5.3. Setting up Your Workspace

A dedicated workspace is essential for running your astrology business. This could be a home office, a rented commercial space, or even a mobile setup if you intend to travel to customer locations.

Workspace Budget: Consider your budget and your business's needs. Home offices can be cost-efficient, but a separate commercial space might be necessary if you want to develop a professional client-facing business.

Equipment: What equipment do you need? This could be as simple as a computer and internet connection if you plan to offer virtual services, or as complex as a fully outfitted consultation room for in-person appointments.

5.4. Building Your Online Presence

Most people find business services online, so building a strong online presence is crucial. This includes a fully functional website, engaging social media profiles, and a content strategy to engage and attract potential customers.

Creating a Website: Work on a professional portfolio website which showcases your services and experience and has booking functionality.

Social Media Presence: Frequently post interesting content on social media platforms where your target customers are active.

5.5. Your Service Portfolio

Detailed service descriptions help customers understand what they're getting and why it's valuable. This could be one-on-one consultations, written reports, classes, group sessions, or something else altogether. Work on developing different packages for different types of customers.

5.6. Pricing Strategy

Your pricing strategy should reflect the value of your services, your projected costs, and your desired profit margins. Consider the prices of similar services in your market as a benchmark.

5.7. Launch Plan

A compelling launch introduces your business to potential clients and sets up early sales success. Plan the launch activities in advance; these can include online promotions, in-person events, or collaborations with strategic partners.

These are the key components for setting up a successful astrology business. Each one represents a step along your journey, and by paying close attention to each step, you'll create a business that's deeply satisfying and successful in the long run. Your entrepreneurial North Star awaits!

Chapter 6. Stellar Services: Creating an Attractive Astrological Portfolio

In the vastness of the cosmos, the nature of your services plays a pivotal role in shaping your astrology business's identity. Crafting an appealing astrological portfolio is crucial—not only to capture the interest of potential clients but also to showcase the depth of your knowledge and the style of your practice.

6.1. Constructing Your Portfolio

Starting your portfolio might seem like a daunting task. In this universe of countless stars and systems, where do you commence? It's simpler than you think. Your portfolio should be a comprehensive representation of your skills, the services you offer, and the unique value that you bring to the table. It isn't enough to say that you can chart a birth or create a horoscope—you need to demonstrate how and why your services are unique and beneficial.

Here are some steps to get you started:

1. **Define Your Services**: What astrological services you will provide? Will you focus on natal charts, synastry, predictive astrology, or a combination? Defining the scope of your services is the first critical step.

2. **Showcase Previous Work**: Are there charts you've done or readings you've given that you're particularly proud of? Maintain privacy by altering the names and sensitive details; the focus should be on your analysis and interpretation, not the client's private information.

3. **Outline Your Process**: Displaying the method behind the magic

can help build trust. Include a detailed explanation of how you analyze a chart or create a prediction, ensuring client understanding and comfort with your process.

4. **Demonstrate Value**: Clearly show how your services can bring value to your clients' lives. Real-life examples, testimonials, and feedback can be helpful in illustrating the usefulness and applicability of your services.

5. **Include Pricing Information**: Be upfront about your pricing. Include detailed information about your charges for various services, any packed deals you may offer, and payment methods accepted.

6.2. Specializing Your Services

As an entrepreneur, you spur innovation by offering something extraordinary. Specializing your services can help you stand out in the cosmic clutter of astrological services.

Consider developing niche services that resonate with your beliefs, passions, and expertise level. For instance, specialize in relationship astrology if you're particularly adept at synastry chart interpretations or perhaps focus on astrological parenting guidance if you have a knack for evaluating factors that shape a child's personality and potential.

6.3. Packaging Your Services

Astrology is a multifaceted field, each element as interconnected as constellations in the sky. Therefore, creating packages or bundles of your services can provide holistic and in-depth insights to your clients.

For example, a package might include a birth chart interpretation, a yearly progression overview, and a compatibility reading. Bundles offer synergy among your services, creating a more comprehensive and detailed offering, and could potentially be a higher value proposition for your client.

6.4. Staying Up to Date

Astrology is an ancient field, but in the context of your business, it's essential to keep current. Your portfolio should reflect your understanding of contemporary astrological schooling and any scientific advancements that connect with or broaden astrological understanding.

Make sure you keep up with learning and incorporate any relevant trends into your portfolio for showcasing the adaptability of your services.

6.5. Collaborations and Networks

Just as the stars form constellations, working with fellow practitioners can bring more depth and dimension to your portfolio. Collaborations might include co-creating content, sharing client referrals, hosting joint workshops or webinars, and more. Such activities display your connection with the astrological community and clients appreciating a well-connected and community focused individual.

Take advantage of these partnerships to learn, grow, diversify your services, and ultimately create a robust, attractive portfolio that draws in your ideal clients.

Your astrological service portfolio can't be created overnight—it's a constant work in progress. As your skills and services deepen, so too should your portfolio evolve. Remember, the goal is to shine a light on your unique services and illuminate the path your clients can take with you. Align your entrepreneurial vision with your astrological wisdom, and the universe might just align in your favor.

Chapter 7. Building Constellations: Network and Collaboration in Astrology

Networking and collaboration are fundamental aspects of any business venture, and the astrology-based field is no exception. By fostering connections with other industry professionals and developing symbiotic relationships, your astrology enterprise can grow and flourish exponentially. Equally, establishing collaborations can help diversify your services, enhance your skills, and add much-needed vibrancy to your work.

7.1. Align Your Stars: Identifying Key Players in the Astrology Market

Marking your territory in the vast landscape of businesses working with astrology is the first step towards successful networking. Identifying key players who are already well-positioned in the industry and have established their prominence is crucial. Such individuals could include renowned astrologers, authors of astrology books, program hosts on spiritual podcast stations, or even successful bloggers in the field.

Connecting with these professionals will not only provide a deeper understanding of the industry and its dynamics but will also present opportunities for mentorship, collaborations, and partnerships that can expand your reach and influence. Regularly attending events, workshops, and seminars in the astrology sphere will help develop these connections.

7.2. Sharing the Same Sky: Establishing Collaborative Partnerships

Once you've identified potential allies, the next step is initiating contact and proposing collaboration. Be clear about your vision, goals, and what you can bring to the table. Securing collaborative partnerships can help you gain access to new audiences, share resources, and boost your reputation within the industry.

For instance, partnerships could include co-hosting astrology webinars, guest posting on each other's blogs, or co-authoring an astrology book. Investing in collaborative work tools like project management software, communication platforms, and document sharing services can facilitate these partnerships and make distance less of a barrier.

7.3. Star to Star Interaction: Engaging with Your Business Community

In addition to the relationships you foster with other professionals, it's equally important to create a network within your customer base. Engaging openly with your community and creating a dialogue will not only facilitate trust but also elicit valuable feedback to improve your service. Forums, newsletters, and social media groups provide excellent platforms for this.

Remember, networks should not just be seen as a means to an end but as a value unto themselves. Building robust relationships with your user community can transform customers into ambassadors for your brand, further amplifying the spread of your mission.

7.4. Building Bridges Across the Universe: Expanding Your Network

With the rise of digital platforms, the world has become increasingly interconnected. By leveraging websites, online forums, and social media channels, you can tap into networking opportunities both domestically and overseas. This can expose your astrology business to a diverse range of cultures, beliefs, and perspectives that might influence your practice in surprising and rewarding ways.

Promoting your services at international astrology conferences or through foreign astrology-themed websites can help expand your business reach and capture a wider audience. Collaborating with international partners might also generate opportunities to learn about different astrology practices, further deepening your expertise and the depth of your service.

7.5. The Power of Constellation: The Collective Success

Collaboration in the astrology business is akin to constructing constellations in the night sky. Just as stars build patterns and navigational aids, business collaborations create pathways to shared success. Remember, the real power of a network lies not just in the number of connections but the quality and depth of those relationships.

In conclusion, a successful astrology enterprise is borne out of meaningful collaborations and connections. As the saying goes, "No man is an island," the same is true for entrepreneurs in the world of astrology. So set your sights on the stars, commence your networking journey and start building constellations of your own.

Chapter 8. Guiding Stars: Marketing Strategies for Your Astrology Service

In this competitive market, the significance of coherent, effective marketing can't be overstated. A strong strategy rocket-propels your brand into the cosmos, attracting prospective clients and ensuring your astrology service stands out. The subsequent, complete guide gives insight into these stellar marketing maneuvers.

8.1. Understand Your Target Audience

The exploration of your marketing journey begins by understanding your target audience. The astrology industry appeals to various segments including the curious, spiritual seekers, skeptics, newcomers, and seasoned astrology enthusiasts. Reaching these varied audiences requires tailored communication.

Start by creating a detailed persona for each segment. Include demographics, characteristics, preferences, and how they use astrology. For instance, spiritual seekers might incorporate astrological insight into daily meditation while skeptics likely need more scientific reassurances.

You can conduct online surveys or host focus group sessions to gain these insights. The information gathered will be instrumental in guiding your marketing messaging.

8.2. Create an Engaging Brand

To stand out in the cosmos of astrology services, cultivating a distinct, engaging brand is paramount. Your brand should be a mirror reflecting your business, values, and unique offerings. Look for ways to integrate your personal expression or approach to astrology into your branding strategy.

Consider your logo, color scheme, imagery, tone of voice, and the overall personality your brand conveys. Affirming a consistent brand message across your channels will lead to brand recognition and loyalty.

8.3. Develop a Stellar Website

Your website serves as your digital abode – a place where interested visitors can journey through your offerings and decide to become customers. It should reflect your brand aesthetic and be easy to navigate. Use the homepage to outline your services, share your story, and highlight testimonials. Include a blog section where you can share educational content about astrology, client experiences, or even case studies.

Ensure your website is also optimized for SEO. By using relevant keywords in your website's content, you're increasing your chances of being found by people searching for astrology services online.

8.4. Utilize Social Media

Social media platforms are excellent mediums to reach your audience. Use captivating images, informative videos, or interactive content like polls and quizzes to engage your followers. Post horoscopes, astrological insights, or personal musings to establish your authority. Consider the preferences of each platform—for instance, Instagram favors visually appealing content, while Twitter is perfect for concise, insightful commentary.

8.5. Leverage Email Marketing

Email marketing offers a direct route to your clients. Consider creating a free newsletter to share astrology insights and updates about your business. Personalize it to foster a connection with your subscribers. Periodically, offer exclusive discounts to your email subscribers to encourage them to avail of your services.

8.6. Offer a Unique Product or Service

In this crowded market, offering a unique service can draw clients. Consider specializing in a niche area like parenting with astrology or astrology for career planning. Alternatively, you could offer creative product lines such as personalized astrological reports or themed merchandise.

8.7. Form Partnerships

Connect with others in your industry such as yoga studios or wellness centers. Offering joint services or packages can expand your reach and drive cross-promotion.

8.8. Track Your Performance

It's important to monitor your marketing efforts and make sure they're guiding your business to success. Use tools like Google Analytics to track your website traffic or social media analytics to check engagement. This allows you to refine your strategies based on what's effective.

These strategies aren't just about gaining clients—they're about defining your place in the cosmos of astrology services. Remember, the journey of an entrepreneur is a dynamic one, full of shifts and turns. Over time, you'll adapt these strategies and find what resonates best with your brand, your audience, and yourself. As you propel your service into this exciting frontier, these guidelines stand as your guiding stars, illuminating the path to success.

Chapter 9. Celestial Scale: Growing Your Astrology Business

Astrology is a fascinating universe in itself, weaving together the celestial and terrestrial realms. Your decision to embark on this entrepreneurial journey is commendable. However, just like the cosmos, the business world is vast, multifaceted, and can sometimes seem insurmountable. Fortunately, a methodical and strategic approach can guide you through each phase of this endeavor, maximizing your chances of prosperity and growth.

9.1. Star Mapping: Strategic Planning

Strategic planning forms the backbone of any successful business. This applies equally to an endeavor as unique as an astrology enterprise. Begin by identifying your unique selling proposition (USP). Perhaps your interpretive abilities are outstanding, or your knowledge of esoteric systems like Hellenistic astrology sets you apart. Your USP becomes your guiding star.

Crucial to your business growth is your target market—your constellation of potential clients. Conduct market research to identify who they are, their needs, and how your services can align with their lives. This could involve online surveys, focus groups, or analyzing existing market data.

Next, outline your business goals. These could range from reaching a certain number of clients, achieving a set income, or becoming known within specific communities. Remember, just like celestial bodies move in cycles, your goals should be cyclic and iterative—think months and years, not just days and weeks.

9.2. Comet's Tail: Branding and Visibility

Just as a comet leaves a distinctive tail, your astrology business needs to develop a strong brand and visibility. Invest time in creating a logo, website, and imagery that aligns with your unique brand. Social media platforms can be highly effective in reaching audiences interested in astrology, spiritual growth, and personal transformation.

Consider offering free or discounted readings to build client trust, garner reviews and testimonials, and boost word-of-mouth advertising. Also, consider collaborating with other businesses or influencers in the spiritual realm. Through co-marketing, you gain exposure to their audience, and they to yours.

9.3. Lunar Phases: Diversifying Your Service Offerings

The moon's phases symbolize growth, development, and change—features intrinsic to any growing business. As you establish your enterprise, consider expanding your services. Besides private readings, you could offer group readings, workshops, online courses, or digital products such as eBooks or guides. Each provides a new revenue stream while enhancing client engagement.

9.4. The Zodiac Wheel: Monetization

Turning your passion into profit involves understanding monetization strategies. One such method is to use a tiered pricing structure in which distinct services are offered at different price points. Also consider subscription-based services, where clients pay a recurring fee for continuous access to certain services like monthly forecasts.

Offering merchandise like astrology books, healing crystals, or star chart posters is another great angle. Co-branded merchandise with collaborators can also widen your reach and diversify your product offerings.

9.5. Solar Storms: Overcoming Challenges

Like our cosmos, business is in a constant state of flux. Be prepared for challenges and setbacks. These might be in the form of financial turbulence, a drop in clientele, or technological issues. Having a contingency plan in place can prevent difficulties from becoming disasters.

In conclusion, with careful planning, innovative marketing, service diversification, smart monetization, and resilience in the face of adversity, your astrology business can reach the stars. Always remember, the cosmic journey of an astrology entrepreneur is a spiritual endeavor of cosmic proportions, as well as an entrepreneurial one. It is a balance between the mystical and the practical, the celestial and the earthly.

By entire universes waiting to be discovered, so too is your potential in this business realm. As you align with the spiritual, celestial map that astrology offers you, your business will blaze its own trail, luminously echoing across the solar system of entrepreneurial success.

Chapter 10. Measuring the Planetary Pull: Analytics in Your Astrology Business

In the realm of astrology, as above—so below. But in the realm of entrepreneurship, what gets measured gets managed. A successful astrology business combines these two principles through the effective use of analytics that measure trends, analyze customer behavior, and help you optimize the functioning of your enterprise.

10.1. Deciphering the Stars: Understanding Analytics

The famous Swiss psychiatrist Carl Jung observed that 'anything born in a moment possesses the qualities of that moment'. Business is no different—it comes into existence at a particular juncture, pregnant with possibilities determined by its birth chart.

In business parlance, this birth chart is factual data, which can be transformed into usable information through analytics. Analytics provide a scientific base to study patterns, forecast future trends, and make informed decisions. They are used to quantify the effect of certain actions, understand customer behavior, measure the popularity of services, and more.

10.2. Transforming Zodiac into Metrics

Like astrology, business analytics reading is an art and science of interpreting raw data to yield useful knowledge. Collecting and analyzing this data is the first step. Tools for this include Google

Analytics, which provides detailed information about website traffic, user demographics, user behavior, and more.

1. **Website Traffic Analysis:** This tells how many people visited your site, how long they stayed, which pages they visited, and where they are coming from. This information can tell which services are most popular and which need more promotion.

2. **Demographic Analysis:** This provides information about the age, gender, and geographical location of your users. This knowledge could be beneficial in targeting marketing efforts and creating personalized service offerings.

3. **Behavior Analysis:** This involves studying how users interact with your site—what they click, how they navigate, and where they drop off. This information can guide website improvements, increase user satisfaction, and ultimately drive conversion.

10.3. Astrological Strategies for Different Metrics

Just as every sign in astrology corresponds to different personalities, every metric in analytics corresponds to different strategic decisions. Here are some considerations:

1. **Traffic Sources and Marketing Strategy:** If most of your traffic comes from social media, it's likely that your audience is tech-savvy and open to short, engaging content on these platforms.

2. **Bounce Rate and User Experience:** A high bounce rate may indicate that visitors are not finding what they expect on your site or that the site layout is confusing. This could signal that your site needs a redesign.

3. **Conversion Rate and Pricing Strategy:** If your conversion rate is low, it might suggest that your prices are too high or your value proposition is not clearly communicated.

10.4. Forecasting Trends: Using Data to Predict Business Success

Analytics provide a plethora of information about past events, but what about the future? Just as astrologers use the past positions of celestial bodies to forecast future events, businesses use past data to predict future performance.

Predictive analytics uses statistical algorithms and machine learning techniques to analyze current and historical facts to predict future outcomes. For your astrology business, this could mean identifying periods of high demand for certain services, expected website traffic, or the possible success of new offerings.

10.5. Gauging Customer Sentiment: The Emotional Pulse of Your Business

Finally, to build a successful astrology business, it's essential to understand and respond to your customers' feelings and opinions. Sentiment analysis, also known as opinion mining, uses natural language processing, text analysis, and computational linguistics to ascertain and quantify sentiments expressed in online mentions.

By monitoring your business reviews and social media comments, you can gauge customer satisfaction and quickly respond to any issues. In addition, you can determine the areas where your brand excels and those that need improvement.

Just like constellations form patterns in the sky, the world of data creates myriad patterns that can give us valuable insight into the running our businesses. Using the wisdom of the cosmos as your compass, and the strength of analytics as your rudder, your astrology business can navigate towards success. After all, as the saying goes, 'millionaires don't use astrology, billionaires do.'

Chapter 11. Eclipsing Uncertainty: Navigating Challenges and Setbacks in Your Astrology Venture

Starting an astrology business, or any business for that matter, if confronted with the distinct inevitability of encountering difficulties and setbacks along the way. Success doesn't appear overnight and often requires maneuvering through a labyrinth of challenges before you see true progress.

===Identifying Potential Challenges

Understanding the possible hurdles you may come across in your entrepreneurial venture can potentially help you prepare for them and create effective strategies to overcome them.

Monetary Constraints

Allocating a budget and sticking to it can be a daunting task, considering the volatile nature of establishing a business. Expenses sometimes balloon beyond your original estimates. Formulating a financial plan that allows for contingencies is a practical approach.

Client Acquisition

Acquiring clients may not transpire as quickly as you envision. This is a common obstacle faced by many startups. It takes time and tenacity to build a robust clientele.

Market Saturation

The astrology market is a crowded one, with numerous services available at the click of a button. Identifying and concretizing your unique selling proposition aids in standing out from the crowd.

Regulatory and Legal Issues

Knowledge of laws regulating our industry is crucial. Neglecting to consider this might result in legal complications that can derail your venture.

===Developing Resilience and Perseverance

Bouncing back from setbacks and maintaining a forward outlook even in the face of adversity is crucial as an entrepreneur.

Optimism

Maintaining a positive mindset can make all the difference. It becomes a motivating force when things get tough.

Adopting a Resilience Mindset

A resilient mind does not see failure. Instead, it views setbacks as feedback and opportunities to learn and grow.

===Implementing Backup Plans and Contingencies

Having backup plans helps cushion you against unexpected setbacks. Your contingency plan should cover financials, operational processes, and client acquisition strategies.

Financial Backups

Maintain an "emergency" fund that you can utilize when unexpected expenses crop up.

Operational Backups

Consider what you would do if your primary delivery channel (website, physical location) became unavailable. Make contingency plans to maintain services.

Client Acquisition Backups

Consider alternative marketing and outreach efforts to ensure a steady stream of income if one source slows down.

===Learning from Setbacks

Our stumbles often make the biggest contribution to our growth if we learn from them.

Analyze

Take time to analyze where things may have gone awry. This introspection is crucial to avoiding repeated mistakes.

Experiment

Don't be afraid to experiment with new strategies. Be innovative in your approach.

===Creating a Supportive Network

You don't have to undertake this journey alone. Cohesive entrepreneurship requires collaboration and networking.

Mentorship

Seek out individuals who have tread the same path before you. Their experience and advice can prove crucial.

Networking

Networking provides you with partners, collaborators, and potential clients. Attend events related to your industry to build connections.

===Staying in Tune with the Market

Stay informed about trends and changes in the astrology business and adapt accordingly.

Subscribe to Relevant Publications

This will keep you updated on what's happening in your industry.

Engage with Your Audience

Interact with your clients and understand their needs and wants.

Companies face trials regardless of the industry they are part of. However, these setbacks are not definitive of their success or failure. The strength of a company lies in its preparedness and resilience to face these challenges. As an astrology entrepreneur, you can balance your spiritual passion with business acumen and successfully navigate the cosmos of entrepreneurship.

www.ingramcontent.com/pod-product-compliance
Lightning Source LLC
Chambersburg PA
CBHW062311290526
45794CB00006B/2762